W9-CAR-711

CREATION
of the
WORLD

igloo

In The Beginning

Genesis 1-2

In the beginning there was God. Then God created Earth. But to begin with, Earth was as dark as night. So God said, "Let there be light!" So He made the Sun. Now there was day to go with night.

Then God made the sky and, underneath the sky, He gathered together huge amounts of water to make the seas.

And in-between the seas He made rocks and mountains and soil. Then He made flowers and forests of trees which could grow in the soil

Then God made fish that could live in the seas and birds that could fly in the sky and animals that could live on the land.

He then made the first man, whom He called Adam. God thought Adam might be lonely all by himself, so He made the first woman, whom He called Eve.

It had taken God six long days to make everything in the world so, on the seventh day, He rested. He decided from then on, every seventh day should be a day of rest.

And this special day of rest He called the Sabbath.

Adam and Eve

Genesis 2-3

God gave Adam and Eve a beautiful garden to live in, which He called the Garden of Eden. He filled it with the loveliest flowers and plants. There were rivers Adam and Eve could drink from, and trees bearing the most delicious fruit. It was truly paradise.

In the centre of the garden, God planted a special tree. "This is the Tree of Knowledge of Good and Evil," He told them. "Do not eat the fruit that grows on it. If you do, you will die."

Adam and Eve lived happily in the garden for many years and made sure that they never ate the fruit that grew on the special tree.

But, one day, a slimy snake slithered up to Eve and hissed, "You really should taste the apples that grow on the Tree of Knowledge. They really are the most delicious fruit in the garden."
Eve was a little frightened.
"But God said we'd die if we tasted the fruit from that tree," she said. "You won't die!" mocked the snake. "God said that because He knows if you were to eat the fruit, you would become as wise as He, and He wouldn't want that to happen, would He?"

Eve thought this made sense. So she walked slowly to the Tree of Knowledge, picked off the juciest, ripest apple she could see and took a big bite out of it. And, when she saw Adam a little later, she shared the fruit with him.

When God realized what they had done, He was angry. "You have disobeyed me," He said. "You must now leave this beautiful garden. From this day on, you must work hard to grow your own food in the rough and thorny ground that lies beyond here. And when you grow old, you will die."

So Adam and Eve left the Garden of Eden. Their lives became much harder, and they struggled to grow enough to eat in the hot, harsh lands outside the Garden.

For the rest of their days, they regretted the time when they disobeyed God by eating the fruit that grew on the Tree of Knowledge.

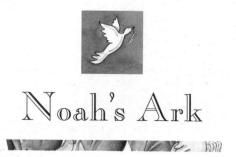

Noah's Ark

Genesis 6-9

God was angry. He saw that most people on Earth were not obeying him, so He decided to flood the whole world and drown everyone in it.

But there was one man He decided to save. This man's name was Noah. God knew that Noah was a good man and wanted to save him from the flood.

"You and your family must build a great Ark," God told him. "In it, you will gather together two of every animal on Earth. Do this and you will be saved."

Noah and his family set to work. They cut down the tallest trees and used them to make the frame of the Ark. Then they covered the frame with rough planks of wood and put tar on the inside so that water couldn't get in.

They all worked very hard for many months. Finally, it was finished.

Noah then gathered together two of every single creature on Earth, just as God had told him to do. The animals lined up and slowly began to troop into the Ark. There were so many of them, it took a very long time. Everyone helped to load enough food and water to last them for months. Once Noah and his family had joined the animals on board, Noah shut the huge doors behind them.

Then, the rains began.

It rained for forty days and forty nights. Soon, the whole Earth was covered with water and became one big sea. The only things left alive on Earth were the people and animals inside the Ark.

For months and months, the Ark tossed around on the sea. Noah peered through the windows every day, hoping to see signs of dry land, but he saw only water.

One day he sent out a raven to look for dry land, but the raven didn't return.

Then he sent out a dove to look for dry land, but the dove didn't return, either.

Noah sent out a second dove. When it returned with an olive leaf in its beak, Noah knew this was a sign that the waters were going down, and dry land wasn't too far away.

He sent out the dove once more and this time it didn't return. Noah now knew beyond doubt that the flood had almost disappeared. He looked out of a window and was overjoyed to see dry land on the horizon.

Gathering his family together, Noah told them the news they had waited so long to hear. Then they sailed happily towards the shore.

After he had made sure all the animals left the Ark safely, Noah got down on one knee and thanked God for keeping his family safe.

"I promise," said God, "however angry I become, I will never again destroy what I have created."

Then He put a beautiful rainbow in the sky.
"Whenever I see a rainbow," said God, "it will remind me to keep my promise. And when you see a rainbow, think of my promise and be certain that I will keep it."

The Tall Tower

Genesis 11

After the great flood, Noah's sons had children, then those children had children, and on it went. Noah's descendants filled every country in the world, and they all spoke one language.

They were learning about things too; they learned that if you baked clay it would become very hard and, from this, you could make strong bricks. With strong bricks, you could build houses and buildings.

One day, someone in a place called Babel had an idea.
"Let's build a tower and make it the tallest tower anyone has ever seen!" he said excitedly. "We will become famous and everyone will envy us."

Work began on the tower. But God, who had been watching them, became sad.
"These people are becoming as selfish and vain as the people I punished with the great flood," He thought. "They have learnt nothing. I must teach them a lesson."

So God made everyone speak in different languages. Because they couldn't understand each other, the tower couldn't be finished. So everyone had to go and live in the part of the world where their language was spoken so they would be understood.

God's Ten Laws

Exodus 19-20

God told Moses to lead his people to the foot of Mount Sinai where something important would happen. They arrived at the foot of the mountain three months after they had left Egypt.

Moses asked the people to make camp and to wait for him. Then he slowly started to climb to the top of Mount Sinai where he knew God wanted to speak to him alone.

Moses was gone for many days. At the foot of the mountain, the Hebrew people were getting restless.

"God has left us," they said to each other. "We must build ourselves a new god to worship." So they collected all the gold in the camp, melted it down and made a golden calf to which they began to pray.